THE QUICK

WITHDRAWN

Lawrence Sail was born in London and brought up in Exeter. He studied French and German at Oxford University, then taught for some years in Kenya, before returning to teach in the UK. He is now a freelance writer and lives in Exeter.

He has published six books of poetry with Bloodaxe, including his retrospective *Waking Dreams: New & Selected Poems* (2010), a Poetry Book Society Special Commendation, and his most recent collection, *The Quick* (2015).

His other books include *Cross-currents: essays* (Enitharmon Press, 2005), a memoir of childhood, *Sift* (Impress Books, 2010), *Songs of the Darkness*, a selection of his Christmas poems with illustrations by his daughter, Erica Sail (Enitharmon Press, 2010), and *The Key to Clover and other essays* (Shoestring Press, 2013). He has edited a number of anthologies, including *The New Exeter Book of Riddles* (1999) and *Light Unlocked: Christmas Card Poems* (2005), both co-edited with Kevin Crossley-Holland for Enitharmon, and *First and Always: Poems for Great Ormond Street Children's Hospital* (Faber & Faber, 1988). He also edited *South-West Review* from 1980 to 1985.

He was chairman of the Arvon Foundation from 1990 to 1994, has directed the Cheltenham Festival of Literature, has been a Whitbread Prize judge, and was the UK jury member for the European Literature Prize (1994-96). In 2004 he received a Cholmondeley Award. He is a Fellow of the Royal Society of Literature.

LAWRENCE SAIL

THE QUICK

BLOODAXE BOOKS

ISBN: 978 1 78037 255 6

First published 2015 by
Bloodaxe Books Ltd,
Eastburn,
South Park,
Hexham,
Northumberland NE46 1BS.

www.bloodaxebooks.com
For further information about Bloodaxe titles
please visit our website or write to
the above address for a catalogue.

Supported using public funding by

**ARTS COUNCIL
ENGLAND**

Cover design: Neil Astley & Pamela Robertson-Pearce.

Printed in Great Britain by Bell & Bain Limited, Glasgow, Scotland, on
acid-free paper sourced from mills with FSC chain of custody certification.

Les enfants et les génies savent qu'il n'existe pas de port, seulement l'eau qui se laisse traverser.

René Char, letter to Georges Braque, May 1947

ACKNOWLEDGEMENTS

Acknowledgements are due to the editors of the following publications where some of these poems first appeared: *Ploughshares, Temenos, The Rialto, The Times Literary Supplement* and *The Warwick Review.*

'The Quick' was included in *The Gist*, ed. Lindsay Clarke (the Write Factor 2012). 'Roman Stone Head' was commissioned for *Making History* (ExLibris, in partnership with the Royal Albert Memorial Museum, Exeter, 2013). 'A Wood Engraving' was included in *Poetry in the Blood*, ed. Tony Roberts (Shoestring Press 2014). 'Another Way to Read Paul Klee' was first published in *High on the Downs: a Festschrift for Harry Guest*, ed. Tony Lopez (Shearsman Books 2012). 'Tidal' was commissioned for the Porto metro. 'A Postcard from the Scillies' was commissioned by Bank Street Arts/Sheffield Poetry Festival. 'Variations on Fauré' was first published in *Long Poem Magazine*. 'Titania, later' was commissioned as part of a joint project by The Centre for Christianity and Culture at Regent's Park College, University of Oxford, and The Shakespeare Institute, University of Birmingham.

Thanks are also due to Elizabeth Garrett, Martina Lauster, Erica Sail and Helen Sail.

CONTENTS

Roman Stone Head

Compacted, hardly bigger
than a baby's fist,
you are of those who have witnessed
something they cannot share

The entire head scoured,
the skin pocked,
but with features that outflank despair
by what they comprehend

You have found the way out
of time to become
undeclined, self-sufficient,
a part that has broken into wholeness

In the Old Jewish Cemetery, Prague

Among the hunch of headstones
one in particular – roofed
with finial scrolls, it has
two tablets of granite text
side by side. They seem open,
as the book of the Law might be
held open

The old, unyielding language
of authority – it presses down,
demanding more than the shade
offered by the trees overhead
to translate any of this
into an expectation
of mercy

Anne Frank Huis

This was the house desperate
not to be noticed, that wanted
to hide in its everyday business
however its tall windows glinted

And this, the crudely made bookcase
beneath a map on the wall
with, slumped in two of its three
shelves, a few tatty files

Too much light came in:
altogether too much was said.
It was too easy to swing
the bookcase to one side

In the beginning, breath –
in the end, betrayal,
along with such words as truth
could still retrieve, after all

From the Lighthouse

At the rough-cut edge
of the land, a megaphone
of light, naked
as distress itself,
blares sideways across
the abraded acres of the sea.

If this were a book, you'd call it
one with a preface and afterword
and a bright ribbon
to mark your progress
from the underworld of the past
to the thin air of the future.

Boat on the Shore

A slow absorption
claims the hull
for stone, even
in the face of the tides –

Otiose, the anchor-fluke
half buried
in the clacking pebbles

Means become end
it is as much
a monument to itself
as any artist
choked by fame

And still a smear
of sky-blue paint
clings to the gunwales –

A coarse postscript
to the last swells
that had the transom
lift and buck

Or a reminder
of the foreword that opposes
the dark running sea
by insisting on horizons
open to anything

At Anchor

Rippling overhead,
its holly lights
doused, the boat
rides under
the wincing stars,
shackled to the tides.

Below, in the roomy
catacombs of the sea,
when the puff of mud-cloud
settles, the anchor
holds fast, almost
as if it could recall
being the emblem
of cradle and cross.

Tidal

From each drowned river
they drain out to sea,
the shivering images
of inverted hills,
bridges and cities,
to be scoured by salt –

and return as stormburst,
sunlight or the moon's
pale versions
of attraction: the flood
of born-again blankness,
a belief in beginnings.

Poème de Départ

Entirely in the mind
like Rimbaud's last voyage
on board a ship
of the Aphinar line –
yet it seems as real
as the smack of the falling
warp hitting
the water, or the way
the hull veers
to face the horizon.

That old trade route,
the course plotted
from the Gate of Tears
to the Gate of Triumph,
won't do – *dévorant*
les azurs verts
shows how colour,
like melody, has been
scribbled across
in the sea's rough runes.

And here, in the wedge
of light expanding
between boat and dock
the prodigal days
of past selves
are soon submerged
in the boil of wake,
the deep shudder
of the engines. Seaward,
the flatlining dark.

Mallarmé's *Sea Breeze*

How sad it is, the sad flesh! And I've read all the books.
To get out! Right out! I can tell that birds are hooked
On being amid the alien foam and the skies!
Nothing, not the old gardens dancing in the eye,
Will restrain this heart that immerses itself in the sea
O nights! Nor my lamp's desolate gleam
On the empty paper that blankness keeps infertile,
Not even the young wife suckling her child.
I'm going to go! Steamer with your swaying masts, weigh
Anchor for the magic lands of far away!

The ache that follows on from hope's cruel spells
Still has faith in the handkerchiefs' final farewell!
And perhaps the masts, attracting storms, will be downed
By the wind, and lie among the ships that have foundered –
Dismasted, dismasted, and never an isle of plenty...
But, O my heart, just hear the sailors' shanty!

Two Island Poems

Leaving Auskerry

Plumose, the wake surged
astern, already beginning
to swamp the view: soon
only an eyebrow of land showed.

Another mile, and the steading
had shrunk beyond beach and dyke,
the yellow-eyed sheep and the terns
subsumed entirely in the sea's smother.

Finally, even the pillar
of the lighthouse with its black frill
of balcony, last glimpsed
between eye-blinks, foundered in sky.

More real now, what lasts
is the island's anatomy recalled
in modest detail: mouse-ear,
blue-tinted eye-bright, cocksfoot, self-heal –

And old friends, that farewell
jig from the figure on the jetty:
behind him, Yorkshire fog
and the countless tormentils' pure gold.

Auskerry is an Orcadian island inhabited by one family, Teresa Probert,
Simon Brogan and their sons Rory, Owen and Hamish.

A Postcard from the Scillies

The land as undone jigsaw, its pieces
patrolled by the oystercatchers' high morse –
but the mind will not be islanded, reaches
away through the flower fields' drugging waft
into a dream of the south, then out
beyond the stuttering punctuation of rocks
to the western ocean, the heave and run
of its endlessly made and remade surges,
where the universal coinage of light
takes the whole puzzle at its face value.

Sea-marks

I remember that ancient look –
a fez draped with weed,
or a light in a black cage
buttoned into the ocean;
and that sizzling instant at which
the boat, gybing round one,
has not yet gathered way
again, or got the bone
between its teeth. But then
sets to, braces itself,
tautens, heels to the wind...
The sudden sense of lift,
of an altogether new
exultation fine as spindrift.

Intervals of 2/2

The ship held
at the paid out scope
of the anchor chain
rising and falling

The relaxed tempo
of the clarinet
on the car radio
fields drifting by

The falcon's awareness
of jess and grommet
the grip of its talons
on the huntsman's glove

The smoulder and glow
of old fire
working away
at the heath's dark heart

Titania, later

There must have been a wall in my head –
with every idea or affection assigned
to one or the other side of it. I thought
I knew where I was.

There were only two seasons, then – one
of moonlit snow, the other of sand
seared by heat. I watched these weathers
build to a climate:

dreams and history, a taper lit
against the dark, accusing words
against absolving blankness, the garment
of praise against heaviness.

Even in the squint dream within the dream
of the wood at night, I could easily distinguish
the ash from the oak, the key from the cup,
reason from love:

and when the divisions became too long
I could always conjure the boy with the arrows,
or his spitting image, the child with his glittering
wound of need.

I thought I knew where I was, in the shade
of the wind-stirred wood, under the moon
that set the tides seething. I saw too clearly
and misunderstood:

what I thought would be exploration
had been there all along, a known place –
as if I had been holding the right map
the wrong way up.

Only at some dazzling moment of forgiveness,
dreamt or bestowed, could I know acceptance
as a true mystery and, with lips closed,
find the way on:

only then could the wall be unpicked,
brick by rasping brick, until
I recognised where I was – and ahead
the land lay shimmering, single, wide open.

Eye Test

Imperfect oculus,
the theatre of the mind
struggles to enact
uncertain twilights
where shapes speak
for less than themselves.

It's hard to answer
the optometrist's questions
as he conjures the lenses
with a flick of the wrist –
Which is better,
with or without?

I allow myself
to think of a drift
of rain, or love
lodged in the eye –
occulting curtains
that are sometimes drawn back.

Anemones

It seems they give everything
in their vehement blaze, the flare
of their glossy petals

In their sheen of blue, purple,
red or white – so intense
that it bleeds from the heart

Solitary, terminal,
black at the centre, they keep
an everyday sense

And persist, until the petals
curl away and the hollow
stems just buckle

Yet their open astonishments
also harbour the closeness
of old absolutes

Of love and grief rising
together from the dark earth
as a single flower

From the earth stained red,
marking where a hunter fell
and a goddess wept

In Absentia

1

Waiting fosters its own complexities –
each object in the house knows
it is more blessed to receive

You imagine her stepping across her room
pausing to adjust a flower leaning
out from a blue vase

You think of the call not being made –
how you might stay hunched in the chair
till the last waver of the light

Or how either one might be glad
of the gift already given, the loyal
and lasting contexts of absence

2

Even the smallest instances
develop a narrative flow
to channel feeling – like
the walk of three years back
on a track narrow as a sheep-path
enclosed under weighty trees

Rare outcrops of bluebells
among great drifts of ramson
that covered the ground entirely
with their deep unsettling waft
and broad gestural leaves...

And already then came the knowledge
of how your eyes would have shone
seeing such wealth – the spread
of all that lushness, the green
bedded overfalls, the tips
of each raised white flower

Those Two

Of all the clocks
those two, proof
against time, return
with the summer nights

One on the wall
at the foot of the stairs
with their give-away treads
and the tall newel

However intense
the dark, it was always
visible in its sheath
of wood and glass

Where the glinting moon
of its disc swung
softly, calmly,
barely audible
between check and release

The other sounding
the quarters from the height
of a square tower
to the south – but halt,

Delayed by a catch
in its iron throat
just before each
last note of fall

It weighted the value
assigned to the heady
silence that dictated
the small hours

Where every instant
was measured by touch,
the slow travel
of hands over inches
of new ground

Figures in Water

In the river Dordogne
an elderly man
stands stock still
against a backdrop
of brilliant limestone
cliff that counts
time in layers:
then, dream-slow,
he wades his way
with arms spread
for balance, against
the quick threads
of light twisting past.

In the Seine at Asnières
the river barely reaches
the navel of the boy
on the right, the one
with an orange hat.
He has his hands
clasped at his mouth,
the way you do
when you shiver – or else
he is calling to someone
he's seen over
on the other bank.

It's hard enough
to avoid the image
such figures conjure –
of a bird or a blessing
exactly aimed,

gliding down
through the sunlit blue,
even when you know
that each is standing
quite alone
in the glittering flow.

A Wood Engraving

(for Elizabeth)

Lavish in the valley of its ripening
the bowing barley
crowds to the field-gate

By the sturdy staves
of the fence poppies nod
to the Orphic dead

And the heart reaches
beyond the instant
in search of immanence

Sei allem Abschied voran
wrote Rilke, *pre-empt*
every farewell

For this single season and always
a brightness inheres
that stuns the earth

Variations on Fauré

Nine preludes for piano, 1909-1910

1

Despite repeated denials, the rumour persisted that the pianist, left alone with the Steinway on the day before the concert, soon had it in pieces on the floor. He was undertaking fine tuning, work under the bonnet – some such explanation was given by the impresario, in a kindly but knowing tone, as if to a child. But the child could have been on her own excursion, returning at dusk with the strangely alluring scent of some herb or wild flower under her fingernails.

Now – and still before any keys have been touched, the pianist seems to want to protect the instrument, at least to hide it as best he can by sitting right forward on the stool, his lanky black hair and the right side of his long black jacket combining to obscure the audience's view. Such complicity! *And under the shadows of thy wing shall be my refuge*, while the black wing of the piano soars above him, propped on its strut. He would like to smuggle the whole contrivance offstage, if that were possible.

And the audience itself has a plentiful supply of long-stemmed roses, held a little unsteadily by worshippers convinced that it will be another evening of pure genius: who, after the assumed encores, will rush forward with their blooms, ardent, their cheeks glowing, to cast their tributes at the feet of the artist, with several of the whorled flowers landing close to the piano's gleaming case.

2

Crackling hailstones beat on the bleared window-panes: agents of spleen. In the yellow half-light of winter, a whole lifetime peers into the room.

Squalls scud across the pocked surface of the lake. At its edge, tuned to restlessness, halyards fret the masts of marooned dinghies.

Brittleness is the rule. At each step taken, the old parquet flooring snaps loudly, like toast melba.

If something is in flight, it must be elusive, more butterfly than bird. Even if it survives the weather, in the end it is brought down, like a kite robbed of the bodying wind.

Night brings a greater stillness, and one or two stars… A time to avoid the lowering sound of church bells buoyed on the darkness; to prepare for the purgative hyssop, and the rejoicing of broken bones.

3

Gratuitously the past will come out to find you, and will find you out. There is no question of meeting it half-way. It yawns open, a drawer stuffed with creased clothes, yards of underwear, tickets for exhibitions, a snapshot of some classical building or other.

Most such things can be edited or discarded, even if it is impossible to tell what might surface next – a teacher's unkind remark, the mad arrhythmia of a long-ago new love, unfinished business of one kind or another... But deep down in the ocean, where entirely new species are still being discovered, the aphotic zone is all echoes, looming shadows, uncertain textures, hints, cartoons: a bull-headed or gape-mouthed creature, with the rictus of a skull or a clown, no sooner glimpsed than lost again as it steers away into the murk. In this place, memory is another mode for oncoming deafness – growing distortion, the loss of certain frequencies and, sooner or later, ridiculous mishearings and unintended puns. Sometimes there is a persistent ringing in the ears, calling your attention to what can only be guessed at.

Explanations are scarce. Why is it, for instance, that a certain Christmas carol should carry the smell of blood, the must of death? What is the connection between the sound of a sneck, with the latch falling loudly into place, and the dire sense of dread that it summons? Such questions leave you as bereft of comprehension as Fauré, hopelessly hearing nothing at the grand concert put on for his benefit. But one thing at least became clear to him: though every excursion might lead from Z to Z, the story of each, however much scribbled across, still hummed with melody and acceptance.

4

Fallible gods, one by one they pass – the tooth fairy, Santa Claus, conjurors, rent collectors who stay for tea, bishops warming their hands on the heads of children who kneel in front of them... For the child, so many disbeliefs to take on! Such lying parents!

Yet the grass continues to grow, to wave under sometimes cloudless skies. In the small garden behind the house, a young girl is turning round and round at speed, with arms outstretched, making herself giddy. Her necklace, a single line of money cowries, lifts and falls against her skin. Her blonde hair whirls in tune with the Hawaiian skirt she is wearing. Hula! The light is as clear as ever after rain. The present is all there is.

5

Dry susurrus of the wind riffling the wheat, close to the roofless but not ruined temple. Who's counting? Do the unfluted pillars add up to thirty-six or forty? If eight choirs each of five voices sing together, how many are audible at any one time? Or are they drowned out by the cicadas' blockading chirr, in the heat of the day?

The sky and the earth with its shadows are as one in the framing stone. Not ruined, but not completed.

Counterpoint has found its way to the cities, with their dusty oleanders and hidden refrains: their endless demolitions and reconstructions, the glittering variations on themselves, the possibilities of danger and excitement.

Yet here, too, are the weak voices of many crying in the wilderness.

6

Even as you read this, three quavers and a semibreve are amongst the opening bars of the music of the spheres, in the darkness of interstellar space where, as part of a diplomatic mission or a grand puzzle, Chuck Berry and Beethoven have joined forces, on an odyssey to evoke the earth. *May all be well...* The first of many iterations, camouflaged intimations of the silence to come. The sounds are no more than sludge, as in the muffle of deep water. But it is overhead where the high Fs of the Queen of the Night meet the night chant of the Navajo. *Bonjour tout le monde.*

The ear attends to the incoming fugues. 'Are you receiving me?' But it is more blessed to give... To one who lives in exile and cannot forget, there can be no giving, only resignation, reluctant acceptance; patience despite the *knowledge that no one will ever say Welcome home. It is a pleasure to receive you.*

The deep tones persist long after the high frequencies have faded, when the sound of the flute and the shepherd's song are nothing more than memories.

No one bends down to whisper to a child the stories of the coiled cochlea or the labyrinth, let alone the astonishing forest of hair cells. Once, it was possible to listen confidently to even the most complicated motet (all those voices ricocheting off the side walls of the canal), certain that each voice and all of them together, united yet still distinct, would make sense. Now it is entirely a matter of the imagination, as it is to think of the surf breaking on darkness, the winds of the earth carried so far. *Greetings from a computer programmer in Ithaca on planet Earth.* And then, in a place not yet even dreamt of, the renewed onset of silence in all its expectation.

7

As if under hypnosis, or drugged, the explorer realises that the direction of travel to follow must be vertical. It is time to abandon the flat surfaces of the Ordnance Survey map. Those views over the lake or to the horizon have been altogether too easy: and even when they are occluded by woodland or dead ground, he has learnt what to expect.

There are some things he cannot help regretting – the allure of the contours crowding wavily on the flank of a spur or re-entrant, close as the isobars of a low pressure area; or the PH of a pub set between green fields and the thin blue vein of a small river.

Even the reassuring shapeliness of the compass rose must be abandoned, along with the figures of fathoms counting their way across the chart...

He sinks peacefully, eyes closed, down through the flag-stones, contained as if in a lift shaft, his arms crossed on his chest. He finds himself wondering what the currency will be at his destination, what new definitions of value, courage and pleasure. Mapping, he knows, is a way of reading the future he cannot escape.

8

Coursing through comes the rush of blood to head and heart, interpreted by the brain as short views from a fast-moving car, fuzzy smartphone shots taken in a war zone and smuggled out. *La main à plume vaut la main à charrue* – pen and plough: if there is a story here, it is the usual one, about getting the women and children out of the wrecked hotel first, or finding the missing body.

In the condominiums of the rich, nothing changes. The gates swing shut or open. The sound of the mower comes to you in strips, tidy as the lawns themselves. Faust contracts the cancer of tedium. In a grey tower, the mountain of light is kept under lock and key.

Before they are shut out by the building at the corner, a precipitation of men in bowler hats and smart coats. They occupy the airspace of suburban Brussels, paratroopers who have forgotten how to fall.

In early spring, a turmoil of gulls caws crudely as they flock in the wake of a tractor working its way across a steep slope.

And here comes the shepherd's hill that once you saw in India: where, if you had nothing better to do, you could clap your hands in the grand portico, and think of someone hearing it at the top of the hill. Clapping before the sun, wind and birds picked your hands and all else to the bone.

In the shrine of the god, a holy mess of vermilion dye, fire and ash, fruit and flowers. A shot from above (taken with flash) of a sleek poet who is murmuring, slowly, *Shantih, Shantih*. And sure enough, almost unbelievably, once again something in the atmosphere or the blood quietens to peace of a kind: *l'abolition de toutes souffrances sonores et mouvantes dans la musique plus intense.*

9

Earth goes through the comet's tail. Two months later, a ship's passenger lobs overboard a bottle with a message: a kind of refrain, a way of settling for now with absence, of squaring the circle of silence. A lifetime later the bottle will bob up close to a hand reaching down, and the comet visit once again.

The parent runs a hand through the hair of the sleeping child: a little night music.

If it can stay in love with the life from which it has turned, perhaps the soul has already crossed the threshold to finding its ease.

L'artiste doit aimer la vie… yet knows as well as anyone how provisional such terms of settlement are. Beyond the chords of acceptance and resignation, lies still the essential mystery. Close your eyes and lips. Think of the hands of the pianist lifting towards the keys, weighted with what they have learnt.

The Earth from Space

Cloudy or clear
familiar marble,
in the dream it becomes
a porthole that gives
from the purely possible
onto darkness

It moves beyond
all argument,
has nothing to declare
but itself, in the headlong
innocence of its traverse
onward through time

At this remove
the unbroken circle
is a perfect disguise:
no clamour of accusation,
and all the prayers
fuse to one.

La Bocca della Verità

How can the mouth
of truth be speechless?
It has become
all shape, set
in a wheel of a face
closer to dismay
than it is to wonder.

The eyes betray
what they have seen.
Between the stone lips
there is no tongue,
only teeth in wait
for the next liar's
smooth hand.

Rilke's *Sonnet to Orpheus*, part II number XV

O fountain-mouth, you the giver, you mouth
that tirelessly speaks what is unpolluted, whole –
you, fronting the face of the water's flow,
mask of marble. And this the aftermath

of the aqueducts, your provenance. Past graves
far away, from the slopes of the Apennines
they bring you to your utterance which then, conveyed
down across your time-blackened chin

spills forward into the vessel waiting there.
Which is itself the sleeper's inclined ear,
the marble ear into which you have always spoken.

An ear of the earth, the earth which converses only
with itself like this. If a jug is shoved in the way
it's as if, somehow, that dialogue is broken.

Simple

In the shuttered house
with its cool white walls
a sprig of lavender

cut from the high
heat of the garden
has been laid out

on the slight rise
of each shrouded
twin bed

blue-mauve
dusted with grey

Salvete!
Valete!

The Whole Caboodle

Clouds come, clouds go. They never look much wrong.

PETER SCUPHAM, 'The Web'

They seem impervious, the pufferies of clouds
that promote the dramatic virtues of gold and pink
or else lay down in blazing shafts of shine
a backing for sky-high gods and angels who preside
over the oncoming swell of hinterlands –
of tom-fool drums, savvy yawning cats,
arrière-pensées, nights patrolled by the dead.

Yet the true wonder of the whole caboodle
can only be descried, perhaps, long after the traverse
of the dark wood, in the dear and living detail
oddly enhanced by distance and always to hand –
the rich articulations of the word rising clear
of dust; the heart's still shocking incompletions;
the rightness of each passing cloud, coming and going.

Two Quotations from Pete Morgan

You granted the poet nine deaths
and, at the end of them, *a freedom
not to have to write, to keep
his poems in his head.*
                And then an alternation
of energy and feline freedom,
but only ever one or the other
till the close of the poet's tenth life,
when the autopsy showed not an empty
pod or husks, but poems simply
unhatched, embryos of the imagination
beyond the grasp of any tyrant,
kept intact right up to the instant when
he turned a corner he had never turned.

The Quick

Not just a kiss –
the unthinking heart,
or a wound tender
in all its hurt,
not just those children
laughing in the leaves,
or the radial blur
of fields seen
from a speeding train,
but like a bird
cherished, in hands
cupped as if
for prayer, and the mind
taking on the tempo
of all that lasts,
all that is gone.

The One and Only

(for Rose)

For you there is no such thing
as any old foxglove –
each new one seen
rings the same
purple bell of memory,
referring you back to the first
one you ever saw.

All fresh sightings turn to
the edenic page
bookmarked in your heart –
the stone Breton house
no longer visited: its garden,
shady and cool, those pagodas,
bee-buzzed, wagging in the breeze.

The Rules

Elaborate but essential,
these are the rules for saying
goodbye to ten-year-old daughters.

It begins in the hall with a kiss
and a hug of uncertain duration.
Enquiries may or may not
be made, some relating
to the day and time of return.

The leaver should now decamp
as far as the front gate,
arrival there to coincide
with the time it takes for them
to race upstairs to the window.

If at this point they judge
your mind to have failed, they will beat
with alarming vigour on the panes.

Stand on the pavement. Stay
in view. Ignore the looks
you may get from passers-by.

Now perform a series
of deep bows (minimum, three)
with sustained over-and-overing
of the leading arm. Look up:
wait for the girls to bow back.

Blow each a single kiss.
Wave with both arms madly,
like screen-wipers working at speed.
When, laughing, they copy you,
it is time to turn and go.

Note for how long you retain
their images. Try not to think
of the rules for saying farewell.

The Woods as Picnic Site

The soldiers hide, having burnt their kit,
the prisoners all come clean,
the flying trickster comes down to earth,
the sword of the king's between
Yseut and Tristran lying unspent,
Uccello's dogs have been put off the scent
and all the babes are sure that the woods are *quite* safe.

Don't believe the TV tales
or twitter-gossip, or the lies that the papers tell,
ignore the fresh-turned soil and the crying
                              of poets who've lost their guides,
'cos the woods really are good *news*.

The Dangerous Seductiveness of Rhymes

(for Grace)

This is the shed against which you leant
at the end of the field, the edge of the world –
this, the darkness only half meant
in which you feared that fear lay curled

This is the crazy, rickety door
of the shed, blue as the summer sky
but rough as the autumn sea on the shore,
the door that gives onto how and why

This is the way to the ferry and dog,
as you know quite well and not at all –
this the acoustic, wooden as a clog,
which will swallow the last of your dying footfall

Weights and Measures

The unfamiliar word alighted
from nowhere in a sweltering Umbrian night –
not spoken, but dream-written
so that I had to look it up
to know how to pronounce it, where
to place the weight – on *o*, as in soul –
eidolon, meaning an insubstantial
image or phantom, something like
the ghost of a ghost.

Outside, each day, a July brood
of large whites worked the lavender,
their mass and movement beyond measure.
Twitching, flitting, flickering, winking,
they hardly disturbed the slender rods
as they homed to the nectar. Profuse as snow,
they kept a lightness befitting the reborn
and raised – imagos, the *a* pronounced
as the *a* in *rain*.

Rain – Somerset in January. It was
in the church porch, as they went with him
over the heart made of slippery, pale
cobbles that the bearers stumbled heavily
under my father's weight, whatever
that might have been. And here is the word's
second meaning – *eidolon*: an ideal
or idealised figure, the *o* sounding
just as in *dole*.

More than One Picture by Howard Hodgkin

Again, the continuum, the track
that leads through woods,
words, the titles
of the decked thresholds –
and who could imagine
that turning back is possible?

Ahead, the dreamed centre,
the sense of it held
within flooding brightness
and rich, dark drapes –
all the colours that ward
the implications of silence.

Another Way to Read Paul Klee

(for Harry Guest)

The joy of little
multiples, tesseræ,
the parts that add up
to more than their sum,
gradus ad parnassum
via terraces of colour –
and to climb is to find
the key to clover
along with other
botanical marvels

Asters that fizz
like catherine wheels,
roses, their hearts
whorls of green shadow
spinning to deeps
dark as any
explored by a poet

And at night, as the violin
conjures a partita,
the nursery letters
left in the toybox
already piled high
with clowns, fish
and cities, combine
in the codes of camouflage,
more ways to keep
the open secret

First and Fourth

(Paul Klee's 'Ouvertüre')

The text has bled
into columns of colour,
with the words rinsed away
into the gutter
leaving just
two uncial vowels
to mark the beginning
and end of utterance

Verso, recto –
we recognise
the pale outlines,
the template of the leaves
that take us, quick
as any flick-book
from animation
to obsequies

But that is all –
a single arrow
points no instruction
except the need
for all appraisers
to invent their own
version of sense
from the ruined screed

Procession

You feel for them, who seem
so stooped by grief, so weighed
down by its first ambush

Their shadows have become unreal
behind their thrown-back or bowed
heads, their veiled memories

They might almost be queuing
for the bread of life, or the chance
to be somewhere else altogether

For the moment, the least brightness
undoes them, they cannot see
the coherence with which they move

As they wind out of sight
they will not turn to greet us,
or look us in the face

From Herculaneum

Two loose hooplas
on one finger of bone,
the gold rings will never
suggest more than they show –

the plain emerald bezil,
the garnet incised with a hen
and her three little chicks

Unlike the fresco that displays
the striped domes of two figs
side by side on a ledge

and beneath, a puffy round
of bread in seven segments
angled to its own shadow

They stay on your tongue – the sweet
pulp, the grain freshly
milled and baked – not salvage
but pale proofs of survival

Relics

They convert devotion
to retail fractions –
a paring of flesh raised
in a chill gilt monstrance,
a thorn boxed in silver,
or the skulls of two nuns, veiled
and with crowns, as if
in honour of death.

But here is the laid out
tunic of Saint Francis,
a map of coarse brown patchwork;
with his slippers, two clumsily folded
flaps of felt. Lived-in,
they harbour a warmth as true
as the edge of light glimmering
in the dark of winter.

Curtains

A pass or two of the hand is enough
to shut the night out and in,
to conceal the star-led wizards, the police
scouring the fields for a missing child.

In screened rooms, seductive conjurings,
antidotes to the ache of winter –
treat your hair with fine perfumes
dispensed in drops, and all day long
cast myrrh and frankincense,
the fragrant fruit of Syria,
upon the soft ash of the fire.

Elsewhere, two bland attendant angels
draw back rich damask to reveal Mary
centre stage, her belly swollen
with the god crouched in the dark womb.

Tree Peony

Involute, clenched, a slow dancer,
it unfurls at leisure its own narrative
of blowsy dispersal

Its petals, silky as feathers, perform
in wave after wave, going on
beyond all reason –

And it opens wider than any book,
admitting everything, its splayed drapes
profuse as praise

Deep pink riposte to the blue bloom
of longing, it offers an exact overlay
of dream and history –

Profligate, yet complete, as if
somehow matching all possible lives
with the life lived

Saint Mary's, Ottery

(for Jess and Stuart)

Outside on the precinct steps,
pale discs, a pulp
of rain-washed horseshoes and hearts –
but inside, netted under
the ribs of the starry vaulting,
nothing seems discounted.

Not the two owls,
the one elephant,
the three green men,
not even
the loud dry click
of the clock that wrongly
has the earth at its centre.

Like the tall iron stands
that offer phlox, lilies
and lacecap hydrangeas to the still
air, everything here
bears witness to the decorations
that belief can still put up,
in the teeth of time – to the simple,
repeated complexities of love.

Jacaranda

An arrested firework,
gerundive almost,
it has long escaped
its Latin roots
to test the space
between being and becoming.

Out of reach,
its intense blue
sky-bursts blockade
the eye – godlike
though tethered to earth,
it strives homeward.

Trakl's *Summer*

At evening the cuckoo's complaint
ceases in the wood.
Deeper bows down the corn,
the red poppy.

A black storm looms
above the hill.
The ancient song of the cricket
dies away in the field.

No more movement in the foliage
of the chestnut tree,
on the spiral stair
the rustle of your dress.

Silently shines the candle
in the dark room.
A silvery hand
Snuffed it out.

No wind, starless night.

Rilke's *Autumn Day*

Lord: it is time. The summer was pure majesty.
Cast your shadow now upon the sundials,
and in the meadows let the winds go free.

Command the last fruits to swell; assign them
two days more of greater southerly heat,
urge them to fullness, inject a last drop of sweetness
into the heavy body of the wine.

For the homeless, no hope now of making one.
For the lonely, no chance of anything better,
only waking, reading, writing lengthy letters
and the prospect of drifting restlessly up and down
in the avenues, when the leaves scatter.

Humming-bird

Small wonder
all of a flutter,
the quick gleam of you
arrives in a blur
of wingbeats, docks
with stillness, sips
the flower's sweet heart.

You blazon mid-air
with a poet's dreams
of appetite, retrieval –
with an imprint of colour
as startling as flying
backwards, or finding
your own voice.

Wren

(for Penelope Lively)

Petite farthing-bird, a single wren
Endowed your garden with song as we sat there,
Notes which lasted no more than minutes, if
Even that. Yet somehow they stay
Lodged in the neural branchwork, emblems
Of every shard of detail that translates
Past back to present, remaking from the faintest
Echo the whole shape of utterance –

Like Æsop's wren which, though not itself
Inured to altitude, still achieved
Virtuoso soaring by climbing aboard the
Eagle's broad back, and in no time was
Lifted high on the shifting thermals,
Yoked to the wonder of the widening view.